Teen Issues

FITNESS

Joanna Kedge and Joanna Watson

Chicago, Illinois

For information, address the publisher:
Raintree, 100 N. LaSalle, Suite 1200
Chicago, IL 60602
Customer Service: 888-363-4266
Visit our website at www.raintreelibrary.com

Printed and bound in China by South China Printing Company

08 07 06 05 04
10 9 8 7 6 5 4 3 2 1

Library of Congress Cataloging-in-Publication Data
Kedge, Joanna, 1968-
  Fitness / Joanna Kedge and Joanna Watson.
    p. cm. -- (Teen issues)
  Includes bibliographical references and index.
  ISBN 1-4109-0612-4 (library binding-hardcover) -- ISBN 1-4109-0883-6
(pbk.)
  1. Physical fitness for youth--Juvenile literature. 2. Physical
fitness--Juvenile literature. 3. Exercise--Juvenile literature. I. Watson,
Joanna, 1965- II. Title. III. Series.
  RA777.K43 2004
  613.7'043--dc22
                          2004015167

Acknowledgments
The publishers would like to thank the following for permission to reproduce photographs:
Action Plus p. **39**; Alamy pp. **10, 10–11, 11, 14, 29, 46–47**; Anthony Blake Picture Library p. **19**;
Australian Sports Commission p. **12**; BananaStock p. **30, 47** (Creatas); Corbis pp. **5, 6, 8–9, 9, 18,
19, 21, 22–23, 25, 27, 29, 31, 32–33, 33, 34, 40–41, 41, 52–53**; Getty p. **50**; Getty p. **28**
(Imagebank); Getty pp. **4–5, 5, 5, 6–7, 8, 32, 32, 32, 42, 43, 48, 50–51** (Photodisc); Getty pp. **15,
23, 40, 48–49** (Taxi); John Birdsall pp. **24, 26, 37, 44, 45**; Liz Eddison pp. **16, 34**; Powerstock pp.
4, 22; Rex Features p. **30–31**; Robert Ashton pp. **13, 51**; Science Photo Library pp. **7, 12–13, 17,
17, 20, 20, 38**; Steve J. Benbow p. **32**; Stockfile p. **24** (S. Behr); The Sport Library p. **16**; Trevor
Clifford p. **16**; Tudor Photography pp. **i, 36, 36, 36–37, 37, 37, 39, 46**.

Cover photograph of a pair of running shoes reproduced with permission of Robert Harding
Picture Library.

Every effort has been made to contact copyright holders of any material reproduced in this book.
Any omissions will be rectified in subsequent printings if notice is given to the publishers.

The paper used to print this book comes from sustainable resources.

Contents

Some words are shown in bold, **like this**. You can find out what they mean by looking in the glossary. You can also look out for them in the "In the Know" box at the bottom of each page.

Fit and Healthy

Everyone feels
differently about
sports. Take
a look at
these comments.

> I hate
> gym class.

> I exercise a lot,
> but
> I'm still fat.

> All my friends are
> skinny, but I've got
> big hips.

> I can't run
> far because I've
> got asthma.

> Sports
> are boring.

To make the most out of life, you need to be fit
and healthy. If you are fit and healthy, you are
more likely to be able to enjoy activities such as
dancing with your friends, walking to school or
to the mall, and playing your favorite sports.

Keeping fit can help you live longer and help to
prevent **diseases** in the future. It can help you
feel good about yourself and make your body
strong and flexible. Exercise can also help you
relax. There is only one person responsible for
taking care of your body and keeping it healthy.
That person is YOU.

> How do
> I know if I am
> exercising enough?

asthma   condition that makes breathing difficult

Fit for what?

When you say the word *fit*, lots of people think of top sports stars winning major championships. Athletes like this train every day. Being fit is part of their job. They need to be in great shape to be able to compete and win.

However, the kind of fitness that we are talking about is for everyone. People like you and your friends and family. It is about keeping healthy and having fun.

Why am I no good at sports?

How do I lose weight?

Find out later . . .

What do we think about our bodies?

How can you fit exercise into your life?

How can exercise help you make friends?

disease **unhealthy condition**

Why do people keep fit?

There are lots of reasons why people keep fit. Sometimes they want to be fit to play sports and be on a team. Or they want to feel better about the way they look. They know that keeping fit can help them to lose weight and look **toned.**

What is your favorite sport?

I was interested in ice hockey when I was young. It was a great way to keep myself fit and looking good. I also met lots of my friends while playing. The only way I can become a better player is to practice regularly.

professional doing something as a job, not just as a hobby

It is not just about looking good, though. Some people exercise regularly to keep their insides healthy, too. Exercise is great for your heart, lungs, muscles, and bones. Lots of young people also play sports or do activities such as rollerblading or skateboarding because they are enjoyable and good ways to make friends.

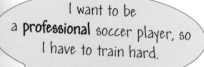

I want to be a **professional** soccer player, so I have to train hard.

I get really **stressed** about schoolwork and exams. Keeping fit makes me feel better. It helps me to relax and sleep well.

I love exercising with my friends. It's really fun and we laugh a lot.

Heart

There are so many benefits of exercising regularly. It can mean the difference between life and death.

▼ The heart on the left is **diseased**. It is the heart of a person who hasn't exercised much and has eaten unhealthy foods. The heart on the right is from a healthy person who has exercised regularly.

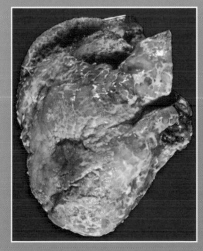
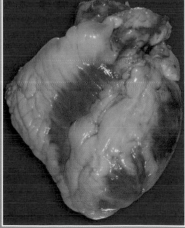

stressed feeling pressured about something
toned having muscles that are tight and move easily

Why do you keep fit?

Keep fit, have fun

Are you bored in the evenings? Fed up with watching TV? Why not join a sports club or go to an exercise class? It is a great way to meet new people and make friends.

I used to hate swimming when I was younger. I remember getting cold and having wet hair dripping down my back. Yuck. But about a year ago, I joined a swimming club. Now I love it. I go twice a week, and I've made lots of new friends. It's made me feel really healthy, and I always feel **energetic** on swimming nights. On a Friday night after swimming, we all go dancing and have a really good time. I can't imagine my week without swimming and my new friends.

energetic   full of life and not easily tired

"Keeping fit helps you lose weight."

TRUE

A combination of healthy eating and exercise will help you to keep at a weight with which you are happy. Exercising regularly increases your **metabolism,** so your body stores less of the food you eat as fat. It also builds up your muscles, making your body feel more **toned** and shapely.

Since I've been taking my final exams, I've felt really **stressed** out. When I study, I just start panicking and feel like I don't know anything. I talked to my friend about it, and he suggested that, in addition to swimming, I should go for a walk. I thought this was a stupid idea. How could a walk help me to feel less stressed? But I gave it a try and I've started walking around the park when I feel stressed. Now I feel much more peaceful and relaxed when I go back to my exams. Hopefully, I'll do better now.

Body Changes

Our bodies change as we get older. If you think back to what you were like as a young child, you will see how much your body has changed already. Between the ages of nine and sixteen, all young people go through some very big changes.

Here are some young people's thoughts on some of these body changes.

I felt so embarrassed when my breasts first started showing. All the girls were comparing how big they were. Some of my friends had breasts much earlier than me and other friends still haven't developed any. Once you know that everyone else is going through these changes, too, it becomes easier.

I felt really embarrassed when my breasts started growing and I had to wear a bra. I know it is normal, though.

Even though I exercised a lot, when I went through puberty I gained weight and my hips got wider.

hormone   chemical messenger that is released by the brain and sent around the body

These changes will happen to different people at different times, but eventually everyone will go through them. This time in a young person's life is called **puberty**. It begins when chemicals called **hormones** are released into the brain. The main female hormone is called estrogen and the male hormone is called testosterone.

Even though I know the changes are natural and it's all just a part of me growing up, I hate getting pimples. My skin is much oilier than it used to be and I have to keep it cleaner. I wash my face, shoulders, and chest at least twice a day to keep my pimples under control.

I seem to get more sweaty now. I need to shower more and wear deodorant.

My friend Peter started growing small breasts at the start of puberty, but they soon went away.

puberty   changes that happen to young people as they grow into adults

Why Exercise?

Keeping fit and exercising helps us in different ways. It makes us stronger and increases our **stamina,** which means that we can keep exercising for longer. Exercise also improves our flexibility, making it easier for us to touch our toes or reach for things on a high shelf. It also gives us more energy.

A strong heart and lungs provide a sure path to living a longer and more enjoyable life. Playing sports is not only good for your health, it also gives you the chance to make friends. Through sports I have traveled the world and seen many new and exciting things.

Tudor Bidder,
Olympic coach

endorphin   natural chemical made in the brain that makes you feel happy and good about yourself

Brain: Exercise **stimulates** your brain and leaves you feeling good.

Lungs: Exercise makes you breathe more **efficiently** and take in more **oxygen**. Humans need oxygen. We cannot live without it.

Heart: Exercise helps to keep your heart strong and healthy and reduces the risk of having a **heart attack** or **stroke**.

Muscles: Exercise strengthens your muscles and makes them more flexible.

Bones: Exercise makes your bones stronger and less likely to break if you fall over.

Energy

Exercise stimulates your brain to make natural body chemicals called **endorphins**. This is what leaves you feeling **energetic** after a good workout.

heart attack   sudden failure of the heart
oxygen   gas found in the air that humans need to live

13

Benefits to muscles

Healthy muscles are not just important for athletes. Muscles are the parts of your body that help you to move. They are usually fixed to the bones in your body by **tendons.** When we want to walk or move, messages from the brain tell the muscles how they should work. If you exercise regularly, your muscles will become stronger and more **supple.** By exercising your muscles, your body stores less fat, so you will stay in good shape, too.

Too much muscle

I thought I would look so cool, having a huge chest and big arm muscles, but instead I look like a freak. If only I had listened to all my friends telling me that it was dangerous for my health to work out on just one area of my body.

▶This girl is doing a spinal twist stretch in a yoga class.

supple   easy to bend

Dear Doc,

I know that exercise is really good for my body and muscles, but I don't want my muscles to get too big in some places, like my legs and arms. What exercise can I do that would be good for my whole body?

From Emma, age 14

Q What sort of exercise is good for all my muscles?

A Dancing, yoga, or swimming are all great ways to build and strengthen all the muscles in your body at the same time.

Dear Emma,

You are right that exercise is good for you, and that it is a bad idea to focus too much on certain muscles. The best type of exercise gives you an all-over workout, so that all your muscles are fit and healthy. Swimming is really good, and yoga is excellent for general fitness, too. Make sure that before deciding what to do, you get good advice from a teacher or doctor.

tendons very strong bands of tissue that connect your muscles to your bones

Benefits to the heart

Exercising gets your **circulation** working well, which makes your heart stronger. The best type of exercise for your heart is **aerobic** exercise, which allows more blood and **oxygen** to be pumped around the body. Popular aerobic activities include fast walking, jogging, swimming, cycling, and dancing. Being overweight or **obese** can put a strain on your heart and cause it to stop working correctly. Being overweight as a teenager can have serious effects on your health for the rest of your life. It is easy to start solving the problem by doing some simple exercises.

Heart beat

Did you know that your heart beats 100,000 times each day and that a healthy heart never gets tired?

Recipe for a healthy heart:

- eat at least five portions of fruit and vegetables every day;

- do at least three sessions of exercise each week;

- never start smoking or chewing tobacco.

cholesterol   fatty substance made by the body that can block the arteries to and from the heart

Sometimes I really hate myself for being fat. I get tired just walking up the stairs or going to the local stores. My doctor says I'm putting pressure on my heart. If I'm not more careful, I will be seriously ill before I'm even twenty. She told me to find an exercise that I enjoy. She also thinks I should eat more fruits and vegetables and fewer french fries and fried, fatty foods. I'm going to really try to lose weight. I want to join in with other people my age and know that I'm healthy.

Why can't I eat lots of fatty foods?

The **arteries** in our body carry food and oxygen in the blood. Eating foods that contain a lot of fat and **cholesterol,** such as fries and burgers, can block up the arteries. Many people have **heart attacks** and other heart-related problems because of blocked arteries.

> > > > > > >

Try the quiz on pages 26 to 27 to see how you feel about your body.

obese   very overweight

Q I love sports, but my knees hurt when I run or play on hard surfaces such as concrete. Is it better for me to play on grass?

A Exercise should be done on soft surfaces when possible. Otherwise, the impact of the ground on your joints, such as your knees, ankles, and hips, is too strong and may damage them. Keep to the grass when you can and play lots of different sports.

▶ The best way to avoid osteoporosis is to do lots of exercise when you are younger.

Benefits to bones

Our skeletons are the frameworks that hold our bodies together. So we need to take care of our bones. A great way to do that is to exercise. Young children have very **supple** and soft bones. You may have noticed that even though very young children fall over a lot, they seem to bounce and not hurt themselves too seriously. This is because their bones are springy, so they bend rather than break.

Some elderly people develop a **disease** called **osteoporosis,** which means that their bones become very thin and weak, so they can break easily.

calcium   mineral that is essential for healthy growth of bones and teeth

What sort of exercise is good for my bones?

As we get older, our bones become harder and more **brittle.** Any sort of exercise is good for us, but sports and games played on the ground, such as jogging, football, soccer, and baseball, are especially good for bones.

These types of exercise are called weight-bearing, because you are carrying the weight of your own body. **Weight-bearing exercises stimulate** the bones to grow, which means they become thicker and stronger and are less likely to break. Whenever possible, though, you should exercise on grass or soft surfaces. Otherwise, these sorts of exercises can damage the **joints** between the bones and cause a lot of pain.

A healthy diet

▲ There is lots of calcium in foods such as milk, yogurt, and cheese.

Food is really important for keeping healthy, too. To make sure that your bones are strong and can grow healthily, try to eat a **balanced diet,** including lots of foods rich in **calcium.** Calcium is a **mineral** that helps bones and teeth grow.

mineral   simple substance found naturally on Earth
osteoporosis   condition that makes bones brittle and fragile

19

Take care of your lungs

Tobacco contains a drug called **nicotine** as well as other chemicals. These chemicals can cause cancer, which can result in death. Smoking also makes the lungs dirty, so they do not work as well, causing heart and lung **disease**.

Benefits to lungs

We all breathe without even having to think about it. Have you noticed that your breathing gets faster after you have been running or exercising? This is because your body needs extra **oxygen** to feed the muscles that are working harder. We need oxygen to **survive,** just as we need food and water. When we get energy from food, we make a waste material called **carbon dioxide,** which our body needs to get rid of. It does this by breathing out. So we breathe oxygen in, and carbon dioxide out. Exercising makes our lung capacity bigger, which means that we can get rid of the carbon dioxide more quickly.

▼ The lung on the left is a healthy lung. The lung on the right is covered in black dots. This is **tar** from cigarettes.

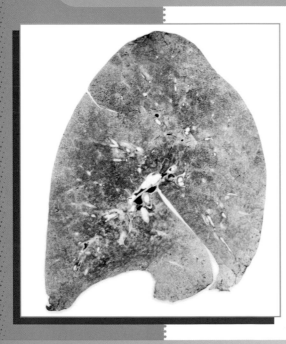

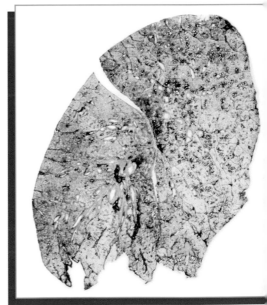

nicotine   poisonous drug found in tobacco

To: Doctor
Cc...
Subject: Smoking

When I was thirteen, I stopped going to my gymnastics club. Now I don't really get any exercise and I've started smoking. I know it's stupid, but I didn't want to feel left out. Now I get tired just running for the bus. I want to get fit again. What should I do?
Jasmine, age 15

To... Jasmine
Cc...
Subject: Smoking

Smoking can seriously damage your heart and lungs. It also makes your breath and clothes smell. Tell your friends why you don't want to smoke. Being different is OK and much healthier. Find some exercise to do with your friends, such as skating, dancing, or jogging in the park. Good luck!

Exercising with asthma

One in five people suffers from a condition called **asthma**. It makes breathing difficult, especially during and after exercise. Asthmatic people usually have an inhaler that they need to puff into their mouths to help open up their airways.

▶ Having asthma does not mean that you should not exercise. Exercise can be very good for you.

survive able to live
tar brown substance that contains poisons such as arsenic

21

Confidence and energy

Kelly's journal

A It is sometimes really difficult if you feel **negative** about your body. How about trying some exercise on the weekends with family or friends? That way, you will slowly get fit and feel better about yourself.

About four years ago, I felt really fed up with my life. I had just changed schools and I am shy, so I was finding it difficult to make new friends. Also, my body was changing a lot as I got older, and I had started gaining weight. The more down I felt, the harder it was to cheer myself up. I would just sit around feeling tired and lonely.

Even though I exercise a lot, I have more energy now than I have ever had.

confident   sure and certain about what you are doing

Then, someone talked me into going to a basketball game. I didn't want to play at first, but nobody was really that good, so I gave it a try. Now I love it. It was good because I could talk to the other girls about the game. Soon, I made some friends. Now I can go out to the park with them and just have fun. I feel fit, too, so I have stopped worrying about my body.

Get dancing

We love going out dancing. It's great exercise and makes us feel good about our bodies.

Yeah, it's good to exercise with someone—it's more fun. Get out there dancing or skateboarding with a friend.

Practicing basketball and getting better at it makes me feel much more **confident** and positive about myself.

Stress relief and relaxation

Feeling the strain

How are you feeling about the dreaded final exams? I'm so worried that I can't even sleep.

I know the feeling exactly. I joined the local running club and I feel so much better. Maybe you should try some exercise, too.

Monday, June 7

Mom and Dad are on vacation. Grandma is staying to keep an eye on us. My brother is annoying me. He doesn't do anything around the house to help out Grandma and me. I decided to go for a bike ride instead of shouting at him. It must have helped, because when I got home, I felt really relaxed and was able to focus on my homework better. I must remember that trick next time I'm **stressed**.

tension   feeling worried and unable to relax

Take your mind off it

Sometimes life can feel tough and stressful. Everyone has times when they feel as if they cannot deal with everything they have to do. Exercise is a great way to make yourself feel better. It can ease **tension** and stress and leave you feeling good inside. This is because exercise releases special chemicals in the brain called **endorphins,** which make you feel peaceful and relaxed. Regular exercise also helps you to sleep better. This gives you more energy for the next day.

How you relax

It's fun to sit and talk.

Since joining the hockey team, I feel a lot less stressed about my schoolwork.

I go to a yoga class. It's great for relaxation.

Body Thoughts

Looking good

I want to look good for me, not for anyone else.

Yeah, I would rather be fit and healthy than look like some sort of skinny model.

What do you think of yourself? For each question, write down a, b, or c. When you finish, check out what your answers say about your image of yourself.

To be healthy, you need to:
a) have fun with your friends
b) eat good food and exercise
c) look great

Exercise is great because:
a) I never do it
b) you can play sports with your friends and feel fit and healthy
c) it gives you a perfect body

What is your idea of a perfect day?
a) lying on the sofa, eating, and watching TV
b) being out with friends, playing sports in the park
c) trying on new outfits and looking at yourself in the mirror

appearance   way you look

How did you score?

Now, count up the number of a's, b's, and c's you have.

Mostly a: You are at risk of becoming a slob. You really need to take better care of your **appearance** and look after your health. How about playing some sports on the weekends or walking to school to give you some energy?

Mostly b: You have a healthy approach to life. You exercise regularly. It seems that you think your friends are more important than your looks.

Mostly c: You may be a little **obsessed** with the way you look. Remember that it is far more important to be fit and healthy on the inside than to look "perfect" on the outside. How about exercising with friends simply for fun, rather than worrying so much about your looks?

Sometimes **puberty** felt like a nightmare. I was so aware of my body and all the changes that were happening to it. I felt more shy and self-conscious. But once my friends and I realized that we all felt a little freaked out by it and that it was normal, everyone relaxed.

obsessed   think about something all the time

Do you exercise too much?

Do you:

- Force yourself to exercise, even if you do not feel well?

- Prefer exercise over being with friends?

- Worry that you will gain weight if you skip exercising for a day?

- Feel worried if you miss a workout?

If you answered yes to any of these questions, try talking to someone you trust. You may have an exercise **addiction**.

Exercise addiction

We all know how good exercise is for us. It makes us feel good about ourselves and it helps us to control our weight. Some people go on diets, while others exercise to achieve their **ideal weights** and fitness levels. Sensible eating and exercising are the way to do this, but some people become diet and exercise too much. As a result, they often become sick. Remember, your body needs activity, but it also needs rest.

addiction   when you cannot get through the day without something

Addicted Athlete

A teenage athlete collapsed during yesterday's race after months of tough training. Sunita, age fifteen, had exercised twice a day leading up to the big race. She even trained when she was sick and in the pouring rain. Her body finally gave in during the race, when she couldn't even reach the finish line. Sunita is now resting at home and admits, "I've learned my lesson. Exercising took over my life. What happened has made me realize that I need to make time for other things, such as my friends and family. I need to take care of my body rather than wear it out."

TRUE OR FALSE?

"You cannot do too much exercise."

FALSE

People can get addicted to exercise and overdo it. They get addicted to the good feelings they get after exercise, just as people get addicted to drugs. They can wear out their bodies and cause serious injuries and damage.

Using performance-enhancing drugs

Most athletes rely on talent and hard training to get the results they want. However, some try to cheat by using drugs to **enhance** their performance. The most common drugs are **anabolic steroids.** They are sometimes given names such as "roids," "juice," "hype," or "pump." They work by allowing the body to do much heavier training and get better more quickly than is naturally possible. They act like the male **hormone** testosterone and are often used as a shortcut to training for long-distance runners and wrestlers. Their use is against the law. Most championships, such as the Olympics, have banned them.

To... Doctor
Cc...
Subject: Steroids

Dear Doctor,
I play volleyball with a team of friends. Some of my friends have started talking about using steroids to make us play better. What should I do?
Jake, 15

To... Jake
Cc...
Subject: Steroids

Steroids can cause heart disease, panic attacks, and even breast growth in boys. Explain to your friends why you don't want to take any and give them some information about the dangers. Ask them to come and see me for a talk, too.

▶ Paula Radcliffe running in the 2003 London Marathon.

acne   collection of pimples and blackheads on the face, shoulders, and chest

The use of steroids is unfair to those athletes who have trained hard and improved their performance naturally. Steroids can also have very serious effects on the body. These include:

- high **blood pressure** and heart **disease**;
- liver damage and cancer;
- headaches, aching joints, and muscle **cramps**;
- very serious **aggressive** behavior;
- anxiety and panic attacks;
- very heavy **acne** on the face and back;
- increase in the size of breasts for boys and men;
- decrease in the size of breasts for girls and women;
- problems with periods in girls and women.

Did you know?

- Some steroids can be safe when prescribed by a doctor for an illness or condition. These will not affect performance at all.

- Performance-enhancing steroids can make both boys and girls go bald.

66 Using drugs in sports is a criminal offense and should be treated as such. It not only cheats other athletes, but also promoters, sponsors, and the general public. 99

Paula Radcliffe, Olympic athlete

blood pressure   pressure of the blood going around the body. High blood pressure is dangerous.

People who use steroids are cheaters. Taking steroids is against the law.

Steroids are drugs.

All athletes should be tested for drugs.

Why should some people take them and others not? It's not fair.

Interview with a male athlete who chose not to be named

Q How many championships have you won?

A Six, but the last one didn't count.

Q Were you very disappointed when you were **disqualified** from the race?

A Of course I was. I'd been training for months for this big competition. I'd only been taking the **anabolic steroids** for one month and I didn't think anyone would find out. I wish I hadn't taken them, since I probably would have won anyway.

Q Why did you take them then?

A I know a few other athletes who take them and they encouraged me. I didn't think I would have a chance if they were taking them and I wasn't.

▶ Ben Johnson won the 100-meter race at the 1988 Olympics. The gold medal was later taken away from him when it was revealed he had been using steroids.

aggressive   energetic in a forceful way
disqualified   dismissed from a competition

Q How did the anabolic steroids make you feel?

A Sometimes I felt stronger and faster. But I got **acne** all over my face and back and I became very **aggressive.** I had really bad headaches and **cramps.** I have a very high **blood pressure** now, and my liver may be damaged. The most embarrassing thing is that I've started to develop breasts.

Q So, would you ever take them again?

A I would never take them again. I've missed out on a gold medal and I have seriously damaged my body. Hopefully I can get myself back to normal, but the damage to my heart and liver won't go away.

Magazines and the media sometimes push people to take steroids, but there are so many risks that it would be stupid to take them.

Taking Care of Your Body

When we exercise, we use lots of energy because our muscles work harder than when we rest. So we need to feed those muscles with really healthy food to make them work correctly.

To get the best out of our bodies, we have to feed them the best kinds of **fuel.**

The food pyramid on the next page shows how much of each type of food we should eat. The foods at the top of the pyramid should be eaten the least. The foods at the bottom should be eaten the most.

I always try to eat well—lots of fruit and veggies and other healthy stuff to give me a **balanced diet.** I know this gives me my best performance. The night before a competition, I always eat a huge bowl of spaghetti and make sure I have a bunch of bananas in my bag.

Recipe

Why not get an energy kick from this banana smoothie? All you need is:

- 1 banana, half a glass of unsweetened fruit juice, and any other fruit that you like.

All you need to do is:
- mash up the banana with a fork or in a blender;
- add the fruit juice and mix in;
- add any other fruit and mash this in;
- stir and drink your delicious smoothie.

　　balanced diet　eating a mix of all the food groups

Fruit and vegetables: These contain lots of vitamins and **minerals** and are essential to stay healthy and fit. They help prevent the body from catching illnesses, they clean our blood, and they make our teeth, **nerves,** skin, and bones healthy, too. It is recommended that we all eat at least five portions of fresh fruit and vegetables every day. Count how many you have had so far today.

Fats and sugars: These foods should be eaten as little as possible because they can make our bodies overweight, block up our **arteries,** and rot our teeth.

Protein: These are foods that help to build muscle and repair the body. These foods include fish, meat, nuts, and eggs.

Carbohydrates: These are starchy foods that give your body energy. These foods include pasta, rice, bread, and potatoes.

Warming up and cooling down

It is very important to do some **warm-up** stretching exercises before you begin a session of physical activity. Some people think it is a waste of time, but it helps keep you from getting injured.

Some good ways of warming up your muscles are walking, cycling, jogging, and dancing. Stretches should also be a part of warming up. **Professional** athletes always stretch and loosen up before their events. Here are some of the stretches they might do.

Stand with your feet apart. Bend one knee while keeping the other straight. Bend until a stretch is felt down the inner thigh. Can you feel the stretch? Switch legs.

With one hand on a wall, grasp the ankle with the other hand so that your foot is pulled up toward your bottom. Can you feel the stretch? Switch legs.

cool down allows the body to gradually return to its normal activity levels

Stand with your feet hip-width apart. Lift one arm above your head and lean over to one side. Can you feel the stretch? Switch arms.

Stand with your feet hip-width apart and your hands on your hips. Lean forward until your upper body is parallel with the floor. Can you feel the stretch?

Why warm up and down?

- Warming up before exercise only takes five to ten minutes.

- It is important to warm up before you exercise and to **cool down** afterward.

- Stretching before and after exercise helps keep your muscles healthy.

> Once I forgot to warm up before I went for a run and I hurt my knee.

warm up gradually more energetic activities that safely prepare the body for exercise

Dealing with injuries

Collision

It is important to warm up before exercising and remember your limits, especially when you are playing a **contact sport**.

My name is Lola and I work as a **physical therapist**, taking care of people who have sports injuries. So many of the people I treat started doing some exercise but did not think about how to do it safely. Often they did not understand how important it is to **warm up** before exercise and **cool down** afterward. I always try to explain to patients that the fittest athletes in the world make sure that they warm up and cool down before and after exercise because they know it is not worth taking shortcuts.

Some of the injuries are horrific. One teenager I treated had torn the **ligament** across his knee when he was tackled in a football game. He thought he was fit and hadn't bothered to warm up before playing. Ligaments are like rubber bands. The warmer they are, the more likely they are to stretch. This boy was in great pain and had to have a cast put on his leg. It took him several months to get better. Think of all the games that he missed out on.

◄ This X-ray shows a nasty injury that happened when a basketball player took too many chances. She ran into another player and broke her arm.

ligament   strong but slightly stretchy material that holds joints together

Pro teams lose millions a year to injury

Injuries to professional athletes cost the teams millions of dollars each season. The teams must pay to care for their injured athletes and could lose ticket sales if a star player is hurt. Some injuries could be prevented by simply stretching more and properly warming up. In all cases, athletes should never be forced to play if they are injured.

REMEMBER: If you have any pain when you are exercising, you should stop at once. If the pain continues, go to your doctor. You may be sent to a physical therapist, who can figure out the problem or give you simple exercises that will make you feel better.

physical therapist   medical person who helps people's bodies get better after illness or injury

How Much Exercise?

This boy is doing too much exercise in a week. He should not be exercising more than once a day.

I've been going running for two years now. I love it. I go nearly every day, even when it's freezing cold or raining. I go swimming a lot, too. I worry a lot about my weight and would love to be a model. I love my food, so I feel that if I exercise a lot, then I can eat more. Sometimes my friends get annoyed with me because they think I would rather be exercising than seeing them. That isn't true, but I do feel awful if I miss my daily run or swim. They just don't understand.

Monday:	A.M.	went for a run
	P.M.	football practice
Tuesday:	A.M.	swim
	P.M.	gym workout
Wednesday:	P.M.	football training
Thursday:	A.M.	went for a run
	P.M.	swim
Friday:	A.M.	gym workout
Saturday:	A.M.	football training
Sunday:	A.M.	two-hour gym workout

I wonder if I exercise enough.

40   **IN THE KNOW**   joint   place where two bones meet

Exercising three times a week for at least half an hour is a good way to improve your health. The body's **joints** can be damaged by too much heavy exercise. These are called overuse injuries. It is important to make time for other things, too, such as your friends and schoolwork.

All she ever does is exercise and worry about the way she looks. She's so boring these days and seems to have forgotten about her friends. If she's not careful, she won't have any left. We all exercise, too, but only about three times a week. That way we have the time and energy to do other things.

Jogging tip

You can build up to going for a jog by starting off with a fast walk. After about two weeks of walking, you could try speeding up into a run.

▼ Start off slowly. Gradually build up to a jog as you get fitter.

Make it fun

Some useful ideas to help you have fun keeping fit:

- exercise with a friend;
- choose something you enjoy;
- remember, dancing is exercise, too;
- above all, have fun!

Building fitness into your life

Do you love being active, or is it your idea of a nightmare? There is one way to find out.

Write down a, b, or c for each question, then add up your score at the end.

How do you get to school?
a) walk
b) car
c) bus

If you had the choice, would you:
a) use the stairs
b) get in an elevator
c) use the escalator

How often do you exercise?
a) three times a week
b) once a year
c) once a week

Which statement best describes you?
a) I really love being active
b) I hate all types of physical activity
c) I don't mind physical activity if my friends are doing it with me

How did you score?

Add up how many a's, b's, and c's you have and find out if you need to change your lifestyle to be more active.

Mostly a: You are very fit and active. Keep up the good work.

Mostly b: You need to try to fit more exercise into your week. Find something you enjoy and try to work toward exercising three times a week.

Mostly c: You like exercising with your friends, so find things that you can do together such as dancing, skateboarding, rollerblading, or cycling.

Q&A

Q I am so busy with schoolwork and seeing my friends, I don't have time to exercise. What can I do to keep fit?

A Why don't you go out dancing with your friends? Or how about walking to school or to your friends' houses instead of getting a ride or taking the bus?

A little bit everyday

My name is Shandip. Two years ago, I was really struggling to get any exercise. Then I realized that there were lots of ways to get fit. Now I walk to school and cycle with friends. I'm fit! A little extra effort has made all the difference.

Top Ten Tips

Exercise is not just about playing a sport. Look at our experts' ideas of how to fit fitness into your day:

- When visiting a friend, why not ride a bike there?

- Going for a fast walk in the fresh air is great exercise.

- Helping your parents with heavy shopping bags will help tone your arm muscles.

- Walking with a friend rather than catching the bus to school will help you burn a few more **calories.**

- Gardening is a great way of exercising. Ask your neighbors if they have any odd jobs for you to do.

- Helping out with the housework at home can be good for you.

- How about getting off the bus or train one stop early so that you can walk the extra distance?

- Instead of using an elevator or escalator, why not use the stairs?

- How about going for a walk at lunchtime?

- Have you got a bike? How about riding it to stores?

calorie   measures the energy value of food

Q How has exercise changed your life?

A Well, I feel better about myself and I have so much more energy.

Q Do you exercise alone or with friends?

A Always with friends, because it is safer and more fun.

Q How do you fit exercise into your busy life?

A Well, I make the most of my time and try to find ways that I can walk or cycle to where I want to go.

◄ Some regular housecleaning can help you get fit and burn calories.

Easy and Cheap Sports

Fit and free

Rollerblading was really fun. i feel full of energy now.

abc 424/1

i loved it 2. Lets do it again soon

There are so many ways of exercising. Everyone likes different things. Some people hate team sports and sports lessons. Some people hate exercising outside or on their own. But don't worry. Whatever your choice is, there is something to suit everyone.

Why not try . . .

Exercise classes: These are usually done to music and are a good form of **aerobic** exercise. Find a class you enjoy. Why not go along with a friend?

aerobic   exercise that strengthens the heart and lungs by pumping more oxygen and blood around the body

Walking: Walking is great exercise, especially fast walking. You can do it anywhere, too.

Team games such as basketball, hockey, volleyball, football: Join a local club or team to play your favorite sport. It is a great way to make new friends and to improve your fitness.

Cycling: Find a park that you are allowed to ride bikes in and enjoy the fresh air as well as the exercise.

Swimming: Swimming exercises many different muscles and is great in the summer. It is cheap, too.

Rollerblading: Go to a rollerblade park near you and enjoy having fun with your friends.

Dance classes are great for having fun and keeping fit.

Exercise with friends

So many benefits . . .

I've made new friends at my sports club.

I've lost weight and feel great since I started exercising more.

Dancing is great exercise.

Above all, make sure exercise is fun.

"Get your uniform on, it's time for class," our gym teacher used to shout at us. This was the time of week I hated most. Getting into those horrible shorts and top in the freezing cold just to run around the school field chasing a ball— not my idea of fun. I was happy when I left school and didn't have to play sports or exercise anymore. But, after a year or so, I started to gain weight. All my clothes felt tight and I didn't have any energy to do anything anymore.

Exercise doesn't have to be painful.

It's a great way to hang out with friends and have some fun, too.

Some of my friends started going to an aerobics class. I didn't like the sound of it, but they told me it was really fun and eventually persuaded me to go with them. I'm glad I did because it was really fun. The music was so cool and we laughed a lot—especially when we got the moves wrong and went in the wrong direction. I go every week now, sometimes twice a week. I can fit into all my clothes again because I have lost weight, and my energy for life has returned. You should try it, too.

◄ ◄ ◄ ◄ ◄
Turn to pages 36 and 37 to find out how to **warm up** before exercise.

Cycling

Cycling can give you energy and be really rewarding— especially when you reach the top of a hill!

To...	Femi
Cc...	
Subject:	Cycling

Dear Femi,
We went for such a great bike ride over the weekend. It's a shame you weren't here. Some of the hills were huge and really tiring to get up, but it was a great feeling when we got to the top. I feel so much better for getting the fresh air and exercise.
Write soon, Joshua

Body and Mind

Feeling great

> I feel great about myself. I am fit and healthy on the inside and the outside. I have lots of fun exercising with friends. It makes me feel full of life.

Exercise can be lots of fun and is really important to keep your body and mind healthy. There are many ways of keeping fit. There is something to suit everyone. Some people like sports and games played against other people, while others prefer to exercise alone or as part of their everyday routine. It is up to you what you choose, but remember to make sure it is fun and enjoy it.

> There are different types of exercise to suit everyone.

By exercising three times a week, you will be well on your way to being fit and healthy. Remember that exercise is not only good for the way you look, but it also affects how you feel. And at the same time, it will be keeping your bones, muscles, heart, and lungs in great shape, too. It is the best way to take care of yourself.

Don't forget that exercise is fun.

Exercise can be cheap.

Surfing
If you live by the sea, try taking some surfing lessons. It is a great way to burn **calories!**

This is *so cool.*

Find Out More

Organizations

American Dietetic Association
120 South Riverside Plaza, Suite 2000
Chicago, IL 60606-6995
(800) 366-1655

Centers for Disease Control and Prevention, Division of Nutrition and Physical Activity
4770 Buford Highway, NE, MS/K-24
Atlanta GA 30341-3717
ccdinfo@cdc.gov

President's Council on Physical Fitness and Sports
Department W
200 Independence Ave., SW
Room 738-H
Washington, D.C. 20201-0004
(202) 690-9000

Books

Ballard, Carol. *Body Focus: Muscles*. Chicago: Heinemann Library, 2003.

Barough, Nina. *Walking: For Fitness and Health*. New York: Dorling Kindersley Publishing, 2003.

Connolly, Sean. *Just the Facts: Steroids*. Chicago: Heinemann Library, 2000.

Frost, Simon. *Fitness for Young People*. New York: Sterling Publishing, 2003.

World Wide Web

If you want to find out more about fitness, you can search the Internet using keywords such as these:
- "balanced diet"
- "contact sport"
- "aerobics"
- "ideal weight"

You can also find your own keywords by using headings or words from this book. Use the search tips on the next page to help you find the most useful websites.

Search tips

There are billions of pages on the Internet, so it can be difficult to find exactly what you want to find. For example, if you just type in "fitness" on a search engine such as Google, you will get a list of millions of web pages. These search skills will help you find useful websites more quickly:

- Know exactly what you want to find out about first.
- Use simple keywords instead of whole sentences.
- Use two to six keywords in a search, putting the most important words first.
- Be precise—only use names of people, places, or things.
- If you want to find words that go together, put quote marks around them—for example, "balanced diet" or "ideal weight."
- Use the advanced section of your search engine.

Where to search

Search engine

A search engine looks through the Web and lists the sites that match the words in the search box. They can give thousands of links, but the best matches are at the top of the list, on the first page. Try searching with **google.com**.

Search directory

A search directory is like a library of websites. You can search by keyword or subject and browse through the different sites like you would look through books on a library shelf. A good example is **yahooligans.com**.

Glossary

acne   collection of pimples and blackheads on the face, shoulders, and chest

addiction   when you cannot get through the day without something

aerobic   exercise that strengthens the heart and lungs by pumping more oxygen and blood around the body

aggressive   energetic in a forceful way

anabolic steroid   illegal drug that builds body tissue

appearance   way you look

artery   tube carrying blood from the heart to other parts of the body

asthma   condition that makes breathing difficult

balanced diet   eating a good range and mixture of foods from all the different food groups

blood pressure   pressure of the blood going around the body. High blood pressure is dangerous.

brittle   easy to break

calcium   mineral that is essential for healthy growth of bones and teeth

calorie   measures the energy value of food

carbon dioxide   gas found in the air. Plants use it when making food; both plants and animals give it off when they breathe out.

cholesterol   fatty substance made by the body that can block the arteries to and from the heart

circulation   constant movement of blood through the heart and body

confident   sure and certain about what you are doing

contact sport   sport in which physical contact between the players is either an essential part of the game, such as football

cool down   allows the body to gradually return to its normal activity levels

cramp   sudden painful tightening of a muscle

disease   unhealthy condition

disqualified   dismissed from a competition

efficiently   doing something well, with very little waste

endorphin   natural chemical made in the brain that makes you feel happy and good about yourself

energetic full of life and not easily tired

enhance   make better

fuel   source of energy

heart attack   sudden failure of the heart

hormone   chemical messenger that is released by the brain and sent around the body

ideal weight   best weight for your body, not anyone else's

joint   place where two bones meet

ligament   strong but slightly stretchy material that holds joints together

metabolism   chemical processes in your body that turn food into energy

mineral   simple substance found naturally on Earth

negative   depressed and downbeat

nerve   fiber that helps pass impulses of movement and feeling throughout the body

nicotine   poisonous drug found in tobacco

obese   very overweight

obsessed   think about something all the time

osteoporosis   condition that makes bones brittle and fragile

oxygen   gas found in the air that humans need to live

physical therapist   medical person who helps people's bodies get better after illness or injury

professional   doing something as a job, not just as a hobby

puberty   changes that happen to young people as they grow into adults

self-conscious   overly concerned about how you look

stamina   when you can exercise for a long time without rest

stimulate   cause or encourage something

stressed   feeling pressured about something

stroke   when the blood flow to part of the brain is blocked

supple   easy to bend

survive   able to live

tar   brown substance that contains poisons such as arsenic

tendons   very strong bands of tissue that connect your muscles to your bones

tension   feeling worried and unable to relax

toned   having muscles that are tight and move easily

warm up   gradually more energetic activities that safely prepare the body for exercise

weight-bearing exercise   exercise that requires the body to carry (bear) its own weight

Index